Introduction to Physics in the Waldorf Schools

The Balance Between Art and Science

Hermann von Baravalle, Ph.D.

Waldorf Curriculum Series
RSCP

Reprinted 2003
ISBN: 0-945803-17-6

Introduction to Physics in the Waldorf Schools

The Balance Between Art and Science

Hermann Von Baravalle

Table of Contents

One or two tunes played on a Glockenspiel* at the outset of this part of teaching will bring the students directly into the realm of sound and of listening. The Glockenspiel usually comprise two octaves, starting from A below middle C. The octave above middle C is included in its entirety. First let the students listen to various tone-sequences. Two tones sounded one after the other or simultaneously give either a consonance or a dissonance. When the middle C is sounded together with the following C, with the eighth tone following it in the scale C D E F G A B C, we hear a consonance, an Octave. When the middle C is sounded with G, the fifth tone on the scale, we hear another kind of consonance, one with a different musical quality, a Fifth. But then when the middle C is sounded together with D or with B, with the second and with the seventh tone on the scale, we hear dissonances. These are the intervals of a Second and a Seventh. One will go through all the intervals within the octave, also through the consonances of the Third (C and E), of the Fourth (C and F) and of the Sixth (C and A).

The Glockenspiel has thus become the first piece of equipment which the students encounter in the Physics Laboratory. The second will be the sonometer. It consists

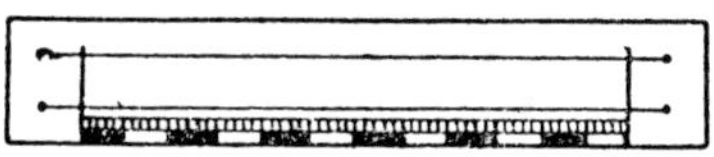

Figure 1
SONOMETER
SEEN FROM ABOVE

Figure 2
SONOMETER
SEEN FROM THE FRONT

of a resonance case on which two strings are mounted side by side. The strings are usually one meter long with a centimeter-scale marked on the resonance case. The strings can be tuned by turning screws. One will start by tuning both strings to the middle C. By using a bridge and dividing the length of a string, one can get other tones from the same string. After trying out different divisions one will

* Called also "Orchestra Bells" or "Gamut Bells."

keep one string with its full length, but divide the other and listen to the interval of their tones. Both consonances and dissonances will be found among them. Then one will aim for specific intervals as they were heard before with the Glockenspiel. How can an octave be produced with the sonometer? Some students with particularly good musical hearing will be called upon to set the bridge and get an octave as accurately as possible. It will be found that the first string sounding with its full length and the second divided exactly into one-half will produce a pure octave. It is particularly instructive to have several sonometers of different lengths made in the school shop, have them all tuned to middle C and hear that all of them, whether long or short, produce an octave at exactly one-half of the lengths of their strings.

After listening to an octave one turns to the Fifth. One will find that the Fifth is obtained by sounding together one string with its full length and the other with exactly 2/3rds of it. This will hold good again with all sonometers of different lengths. As a next interval one may take up the Fourth. The corresponding position of the bridge will be at the point of 75 centimeters, at 3/4 of one meter. For the Sixth the position will be at 60 centimeters, at 3/5 of the total length. The Third is sounded when the bridge is at the mark of 80 cm., at 4/5 of the total length. All sonometers will furnish the same fractions. All these intervals are consonances.

With the Glockenspiel the students had also listened to the dissonances of the Second and of the Seventh. The same intervals will be heard on the sonometer with the bridge at the fractions of 8/9 and 8/15 of the full length. The series of the fractions for all the intervals within the octave is:

C	D	E	F	G	A	B	C
PRIME	SECOND	THIRD	FOURTH	FIFTH	SIXTH	SEVENTH	OCTAVE
1	$\frac{8}{9}$	$\frac{4}{5}$	$\frac{3}{4}$	$\frac{2}{3}$	$\frac{3}{5}$	$\frac{8}{15}$	$\frac{1}{2}$

The smaller the numbers in the fractions, the simpler the fractions, the more perfect the consonances. A way to obtain their sequence arithmetically in the order from the smallest to the larger numbers is as follows: One starts with the beginning and the end of the series, with 1 and ½ and writes both numbers in form of fractions: $\frac{1}{1}$ and $\frac{1}{2}$. Then one adds the numerators and adds the denominators $\frac{1+1}{1+2} = \frac{2}{3}$ and gets the fraction of the Fifth. The procedure (which could not be used to obtain a sum of fractions) is continued for the 3 fractions: $\frac{1}{1}\ \frac{2}{3}\ \frac{1}{2}$. Adding the numerators and the denominators of neighboring fractions one obtains $\frac{1+2}{1+3} = \frac{3}{4}$ the fraction of the Fourth and $\frac{2+1}{3+2} = \frac{3}{5}$ the fraction of the Sixth. Thus one has arrived so far at the sequence: $\frac{1}{1}\ \frac{3}{4}\ \frac{2}{3}\ \frac{3}{5}\ \frac{1}{2}$. In the numerators as well as denominators, the numbers do not extend beyond five. If this limit is exceeded the corresponding intervals will no longer be consonances. Only in one instance one can continue adding numerators and denominators of neighboring fractions and still remain within the range of the numbers 1 to 5. It is with $\frac{1}{1}$ and $\frac{3}{4}$: $\frac{1+3}{1+4} = \frac{4}{5}$ and leads to the fraction of the Third. With it the fractions are

$$\frac{1}{1}\ \frac{4}{5}\ \frac{3}{4}\ \frac{2}{3}\ \frac{3}{5}\ \frac{1}{2} \quad \text{and}$$

C E F G A C

comparing with the complete sequence of all intervals within the octave: $\frac{1}{1}\ \frac{8}{9}\ \frac{4}{5}\ \frac{3}{4}\ \frac{2}{3}\ \frac{3}{5}\ \frac{8}{15}\ \frac{1}{2}$ there are only missing $\frac{8}{9}$ and $\frac{8}{15}$, the fractions after the beginning and before the end, the fractions of the Second and of the Seventh, the two intervals of dissonances. These fractions have numerators of 8. If we also write the first and the last fractions for comparative purposes with numerators of 8, we obtain $\frac{1}{1} = \frac{8}{8}$ and $\frac{1}{2} = \frac{8}{16}$. The fraction of the Second, $\frac{8}{9}$, has a denominator of One above the denominator of $\frac{8}{8}$

and the fraction of the Seventh, $\frac{8}{15}$, has a denominator of One below the denominator of $\frac{8}{16}$. The intervals of dissonances complete the series. Both consonances and dissonances have their parts within the totality of the musical scale.

The experiments with the sonometers can be continued with other devices, for instance two glass cylinders of the same size. First the cylinders are empty. One blows from the side over their openings and a certain tone is heard. Then, leaving one of the two cylinders empty the other is partly filled with water. By blowing over its opening different tones can be produced. The more water is poured into the cylinder the higher its tone becomes. Making the second cylinder exactly half full and blowing again over its opening, one obtains precisely the interval of an octave of the cylinder. Just as the octave had been obtained with the strings of the sonometer of the whole length and one-half of it, so also an octave is obtained with the full air space of a cylinder and one-half of it. With the other intervals similar experiments can be made. The latter can be extended to the block flute. One also meets them in daily life. Whenever we simply fill a glass with water under a faucet we hear the continuing rising of its tone.

Another means of experimenting with musical intervals is the use of cardboard rolls. Holding such a roll freely in the hand and blowing from the side over one of its ends, one will hear a tone. Another roll of a different length will give another tone. The shorter the roll the higher is the tone, and the longer the roll the deeper the tone. If one takes two rolls, one double the size of the other, one gets an octave between their tones. With a series of rolls, adjusted in their respective lengths to the fractions of the musical intervals, one can reproduce the whole scale. Even sheets of paper loosely rolled together can be used to the same end.

Regarding the octave one does not even need two cardboard-paper rolls. One can take one cardboard roll, hold it with both hands, with one in the middle and with the other closing its lower opening, while blowing over the other end. After removing the closing hand, one blows again. The tone will change to exactly one octave higher. From the octave as a musical experience one has thus arrived at the octave as related to a ratio and finally to the octave as produced by a simple change in manipulating a cardboard roll.

Another device for experimenting with the musical intervals is a rotating acoustic disc. The disc is mounted on a whirling table and usually contains four series of holes distributed at equal distances around the circumferences of concentric circles. The numbers of the holes usually are 24 30 36 and 48. By holding the corner of a visting card at the rotating disc against one of the concentric circles, a tone will be heard. The more holes a circle contains, the higher the tone. The circles with 24 holes and with 48 holes with their ratios: $\frac{48}{24} = 2$ or $\frac{24}{48} = \frac{1}{2}$ give an octave. The circles of 24 and 36 holes with their ratios $\frac{36}{24} = \frac{3}{2}$ or $\frac{24}{36} = \frac{2}{3}$ produce a Fifth between them. The circles of 24 and of 30 holes with their ratios $\frac{30}{24} = \frac{5}{4}$ or $\frac{24}{30} = \frac{4}{5}$ give a Third etc.

On the edge of the disc there are often teeth cut out like a saw. By rotating the disc and holding a visiting card loosely against its edge a tone will be heard. If the number of teeth is 90, the ratios between 90 and the number of holes on the inner circle of 30 are $\frac{90}{30} = 3$ or $\frac{30}{90} = \frac{1}{3}$. The latter fraction can be written as $\frac{1}{3} = \frac{2}{3} \times \frac{1}{2}$ containing the fractions of an octave (1/2) and of a Fifth (2/3). One obtains the interval of a Fifth of an octave.

The nature of the fractions of the musical intervals can be further investigated through the ratios between successive fractions. The ratio of the fractions of G and F for instance is:

$$\frac{\frac{2}{3}}{\frac{3}{4}} = \frac{2 \times 4}{3 \times 3} = \frac{8}{9}\ .$$

Pursuing this through the whole of the musical scale one obtains from the fractions of the musical scale:

$$1 \quad \frac{8}{9} \quad \frac{4}{5} \quad \frac{3}{4} \quad \frac{2}{3} \quad \frac{3}{5} \quad \frac{8}{15} \quad \frac{1}{2}$$

the ratios of successive fractions

$$\frac{8}{9} \quad \frac{9}{10} \quad \frac{15}{16} \quad \frac{8}{9} \quad \frac{9}{10} \quad \frac{8}{9} \quad \frac{15}{16}$$

They show three different values: The value $\frac{8}{9}$ appears three times, $\frac{9}{10}$ twice and $\frac{15}{16}$ also twice. If one combines these three values, in order to compare them, the common denominator is 720, and we obtain: $\frac{8}{9} = \frac{640}{720}$ $\frac{9}{10} = \frac{648}{720}$ $\frac{15}{16} = \frac{675}{720}$. Of the three numerators 640, 648, and 675, the first two are closer to one another (difference 8) whereas the third is considerably farther apart (differences 35 and 27). The fraction $\frac{675}{720}$ lies nearer to $\frac{720}{720} = 1$ than $\frac{640}{720}$ and $\frac{648}{720}$. The value 1 means for an interval no change of the tone. The fractions $\frac{8}{9} = \frac{640}{720}$ and $\frac{9}{10} = \frac{648}{720}$ being considerably farther away from $\frac{720}{720}$ mean greater changes of the tone. They are called the fractions of a full tone interval in contrast to $\frac{15}{16} = \frac{675}{720}$, the fraction of a half-tone interval. Using these terms we obtain the following sequence:

$\frac{8}{9}$	$\frac{9}{10}$	$\frac{15}{16}$	$\frac{8}{9}$	$\frac{9}{10}$
FULL-TONE	FULL-TONE	HALF-TONE	FULL-TONE	FULL-TONE
$\frac{8}{9}$	$\frac{15}{16}$			
FULL-TONE	HALF-TONE			

FULL-TONE HALF-TONE

This has its expression in the keyboard of a piano. The full-tone intervals have black keys between them, whereas the half-tone intervals have none (Figure 3).

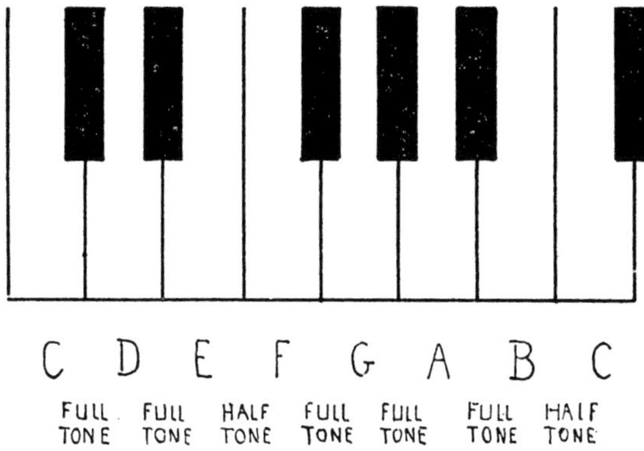

Figure 3
THE KEYBOARD OF A PIANO

The same sequence lies at the basis of all major keys in music. The keys differ in regard to their starting points. This can be followed up with the aid of a self-made paper device. One sets up a scale in which the full-tone and the half-tone intervals are represented by full inches and half-inches. Along the edge of a paper one sets up the sequence:

1 INCH 1 INCH 1/2 INCH 1 INCH 1 INCH 1 INCH 1/2 INCH twice, corresponding to 2 octaves. The same sequence is marked once more on a strip of paper to be placed alongside the paper edge and meant to slide along it (Figure 4).

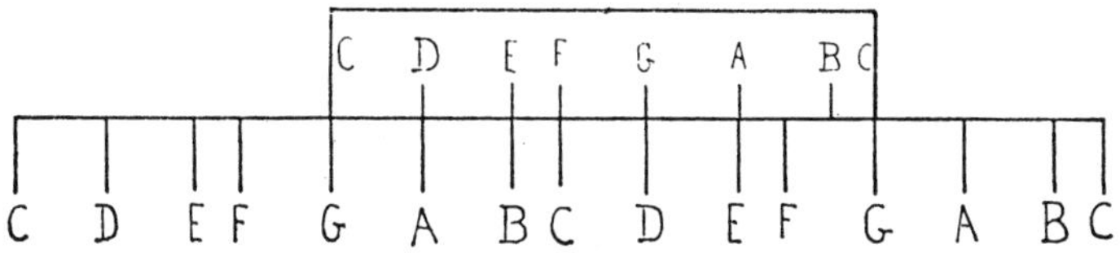

Figure 4
THE KEY OF G MAJOR

If the movable strip is set up with its mark of C coinciding with a C on the other scale, all marks of the two scales naturally will coincide. At any other setting this will no longer be the case; there will always be some discrepancies. With some positions there will be more marks of the two scales coinciding with one another and with others less. By experimenting with various positions of the sliding strip one will find maximums of discrepancies and also minimums. Two positions will be found with only one single discrepancy. They are those positions with the C of the sliding scale on F or on G of the other. Figure 4 shows the case of G and Figure 5 of F. In Figure 4 the discrepancy appears with the B on the sliding scale and the F on the other. The B of the sliding scale is located to the right of the F in the other. The direction from left to right represents the direction from lower to higher tones. Therefore the fact can be summed up as: In the movable scale the tone F has been moved up a half-tone interval or F has changed to F sharp and is written in staff notation with a cross on the line of F. The beginning of the movable scale is at G and therefore one speaks of G Major.

In Figure 5 the sliding scale is placed with its beginning at F of the other. A discrepancy occurs between the F of the sliding scale and the B of the other. The sliding scale

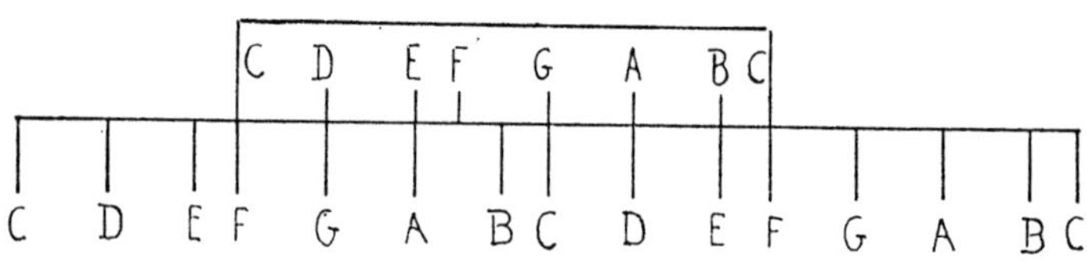

Figure 5
THE KEY OF F MAJOR

has its mark of F further to the left as has the B in the other. One sums up again: The B has moved down a one-half tone interval or B has been changed to B Flat and one writes *b* on the line of B. The key is called F Major.

One can go on experimenting with the sliding scale and find a position with two discrepancies. It occurs when the beginning of the sliding scale is placed on D of the other. The two discrepancies are at F and at C of the other scale. The respective marks of the sliding scale are to their right. The fact is expressed as F and C being raised to F

Sharp and C Sharp and is written in staff notation with two crosses on the lines of F and C. The Key is D Major.

Proceeding this way to 3, 4, 5 and even 6 discrepancies one finally arrives at the following tabulations:

SHARP KEYS

Key	Amount of Crosses	Sharp	Staff Notation
C Major	0	-	
G Major	1	F	
D Major	2	F C	
A Major	3	F C G	
E Major	4	F C G D	
B Major	5	F C G D A	
F-Sharp Major	6	F C G D A E	

Thus an entry to the keys has been found with which their musical structure can be re-invented. The keys no longer present themselves as something to be merely accepted, but as accessible to experiment and understanding.

Further sides of acoustics can be opened up with the following experiment. One places two beakers of the same size on the table, one near the other. One beaker is intact and the other has a minor crack, but so that this will not be immediately apparent. Then one will strike slightly against the first beaker and the students will listen to its bell-like tone. One will repeat it several times, striking at different points. Wherever the beaker is touched there again will be its bell-like tone. Then one will strike at the other beaker

FLAT KEYS

Key	Amount of Flats	Tones Flat	Staff Notation
C Major	0	-	
F Major	1	B	
B-Flat Major	2	B E	
E-Flat Major	3	B E A	
A-Flat Major	4	B E A D	
D-Flat Major	5	B E A D G	
G-Flat Major	6	B E A D G C	

and wherever it will be touched there will be only a broken tone, completely without any bell-like quality. The tone reveals the condition of the beaker as a totality, irrespective of where it is struck. We will find that tones tell the conditions of different objects in everyday life. A piece of pottery is tested with the knuckle of a finger and the Italian merchant flips a coin on his marble table to test the coins by their sounds. One knocks against the wall to find where one will hang a picture, and listens to the motor of a car to check whether it needs some attention. The listening to music thus has been gradually extended to listening on many occasions to non-musical sounds and the acoustics unit ends up with the students having gained a new understanding of tones and a new consciousness in listening.

OPTICS OF COLOR

Take a brush full of yellow water color and place it on a sheet of white paper. Then take a brush full of sky-blue water color and place it also on the paper, at the side of the yellow. Then let the yellow and the blue gradually expand on the paper. Where they come together, they produce green. One will have side by side on the paper: the yellow, the green, and the blue. Then one will proceed in the same way with yellow and red resulting in orange. With red and blue one will obtain a violet. From the three colors yellow, red and blue, three others are derived, green, orange and violet. The first three colors could never have been obtained through mixing; they have to be ready in a paint set and are called primary colors. The other colors which one obtains through mixing two of the primary colors are called secondary colors.

On a second sheet of paper place another brush full of yellow. Recall the change that a yellow would undergo if it were the color of a cloth or dress or curtain and part of it were in shadow. Place some violet color, less concentrated than the yellow, on the paper at the side of the yellow and let the two colors come together. The yellow will appear as if it were in shadow. If the violet were stronger the resulting color would no longer be yellow, but turn to violet itself. Mixing some black into the yellow would not produce the shadow-color. Only a dirty yellow would come of it, not a clean yellow set into shadow. Red mixed into yellow makes it orange, blue mixed into it makes it green, some violet mixed into it turns the yellow into the shadow-color. The latter procedure is called the breaking of the yellow and the color by which this is effected is its complementary color. One is dealing here with a mutual relationship. Yellow is broken by violet and violet by yellow. To have a blue change into its shadow-color one mixes some orange into it. To break red, one mixes some green with it and again vice versa.

All of these color relationships can be demonstrated on a sheet of paper and then summed up in the scheme of the Color-Circle (Figure 6).

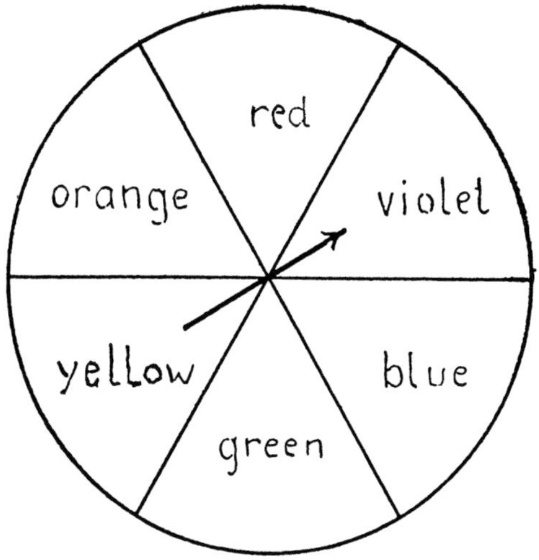

Figure 6
COLOR CIRCLE

The Color Circle lists the three primary colors, yellow, red and blue, and the three secondary colors, orange, violet and green. The latter are placed in between the primary colors from which they are derived:

Orange—between yellow and red
Violet—between red and blue
Green—between yellow and blue

By drawing an arrow in the color circle from the field of yellow through the center to the opposite side, it will reach the field of violet—its complimentary color. The same holds good for any other color. Also other interesting effects can be discovered by using the color circle. For a yellow with an orange tinge we draw the arrow from the yellow field, but from its side towards the orange. The head of the arrow on the other side of the center of the circle will be in the violet field, but nearer to the blue. We read from it: The complementary color of a yellow with an orange tinge is a bluish-violet. Every shade of yellow has a specific shade of violet as its complementary color and the same applies to all colors.

For the next experiments we suggest using a large pneumatic trough or an aquarium filled with water. First dip a brush full of yellow paint into the water. As soon as the brush touches the surface of the water a drop of paint will pass into it and spread, forming veils of color. Next take a brush full of blue color and touch another point of the surface, about three inches from the yellow. The blue color will again sink into the water and spread. When the veils of the yellow and of the blue come together, they produce green between them. Similar experiments can be carried out with yellow and red and with red and blue. Then one might also try some complimentary colors—let drops of yellow and violet sink into the water side by side. Repeat the experiment with red and green, as well as with orange and blue. For the students of this age with their great receptivity for all the details of experiments, it will mean much to see these experiments carried out with the finest quality of colors and good lighting, either natural or artificial. The color-veils, their spreading in the water and the forming of new colors will create a lasting impression.

The next experiments will require a slide projector and some colored glasses. Pieces of colored cellophane held between cover glasses can take the place of colored glass. The colored glasses can be used two ways. One way is to hold them before the objective lens of the projector. This produces diffuse color projections on the screen. When one holds first one colored glass before the objective lens and then gradually moves in another, one will see the continuous change from the first color to the mixed color on the screen. The second way consists in the use of colored glass in the place of slides. The slide carrier is taken out and a colored glass is held in its place from one side. Another colored glass is gradually moved in from the other side. On the screen both glasses will be seen, sharply outlined. Where they overlap, the mixing of their colors is apparent. One will see both component colors and the resultant color side by side on the screen. Again, try the mixing of yellow+blue, of red+yellow, and blue+red. The results will be the same as those of the previous demonstrations. It was the delicacy of the colors which predominated when the colors mixed in the water, this time it is their brilliancy.

These experiments may be followed by another series using colored crepe paper. A string should be fixed across the screen to have one or several rolls of crepe paper hung over the string. The mixing of colors, as well as experiments with complementary colors can now be carried out between the colored light from the projector and the colors of the crepe paper. A yellow crepe paper with blue light from the projector will produce green and the surrounding part of the screen will show the blue light from the projector. A crepe paper of intensive red with green light from the projector will seem almost black, demonstrating again the effect of complementary colors. If rolls of differently colored crepe paper are unrolled while colored lights are projected on them, in the absence of any white light, one provides the challenge of telling the true colors of the paper rolls. When the white light is finally switched on, the answers can be checked. These experiments can be varied by using colored ribbons or veils and all sorts of colored materials.

Particularly valuable experiments involving complementary colors are those that make use of colored shadows. A color—for instance red—is projected on the screen in a darkened room. If one steps to the side of the screen and holds an arm and hand before it, about three feet before the screen, the shadow of the arm and hand will appear black on the screen. Now if the white lights in the room are switched on, the same shadows no longer appear in black, but in the complementary color of the red light of the projector, in green. If green light is projected, the shadows will be red. With yellow light the effect will be violet and with violet light, yellow. With orange light the effect will be blue and with blue light, orange. Two different kinds of green will give two kinds of red, etc. Every variation of a color has its corresponding complementary color.

By using the light of one bulb only, instead of the lights of the room, and placing the bulb to the side of the screen, one will get two shadows of the arm and hand, one from the red light of the projector in green, and the other from the white bulb in red. Thus both complementary colors are seen side by side on the screen. Similar demonstrations can be repeated using various colors.

After these experiments color relationships may be discussed as they appear in our surroundings. Recall the striking color transformation which occurs at sunset when the white light of the sun gradually changes to yellow and red. The transformation is caused by the atmosphere. At different times of the day the length of the path of the sunlight through the atmosphere varies. At mid-day with a steeper angle of the light, there are only a few miles to be transversed. At sunset the number of miles at the light's flat angle is many times as great. A classroom demonstration of this very color change can be produced in the following manner: A pneumatic trough is filled with clear water and a projector is placed at its side so that its light will pass through the trough and on to a screen where it will appear as a circle of white light. As the water is gradually made soapy the white circle will first become yellow and later red.

When we travel into different countries we observe distinct changes in the blue of the sky. Warmer climates show a darker blue sky, whereas in the Scandinavian countries, for example, the sky is light blue. At higher altitudes the blue of the sky is darker. Going up in a plane the blue of the sky gets darker and darker the higher one goes. Looking straight up from the ground, one will see that the blue of the sky appears darker than it does along the horizon. These are again the influences of the atmosphere. Whenever we look up into the blue sky, we look towards the black interstellar space. Were there no change through the atmosphere we would see the sky as black and the sun shining out of this black sky. The more of the atmosphere that is interposed, the more the color of the sky turns towards blue and finally approaches white. The same atmosphere which turns the white light of the sun into yellow and red at sunset time effects the turning of the darkness of the sky into blue. A corresponding classroom demonstration can be carried out with the same equipment that had been used for the sunset colors. Looking into the water of a trough with the light of the projector passing through it, and this time looking in a direction perpendicular to the direction of the light, and through the illuminated water towards a dark background, one will notice the color blue appear in the first beginning of the water's being made soapy, and the color will change from dark blue to lighter sky blue as the soap content increases. Having both demonstrations, the one of the sunset colors and the one of the blue carried out with the same water and the same soap renders it clear that the colors do not come from the soap itself. The experiments provide much opportunity to stimulate detailed color observation.

Finally, one would add demonstrations of colors produced with the aid of a prism. The larger size projector—for 3¼ x 4″ slides is most satisfactory for this. For these experiments a projector should be placed in a darkened room, in front of the class, but to one side of the demonstration table. (Figure 7)

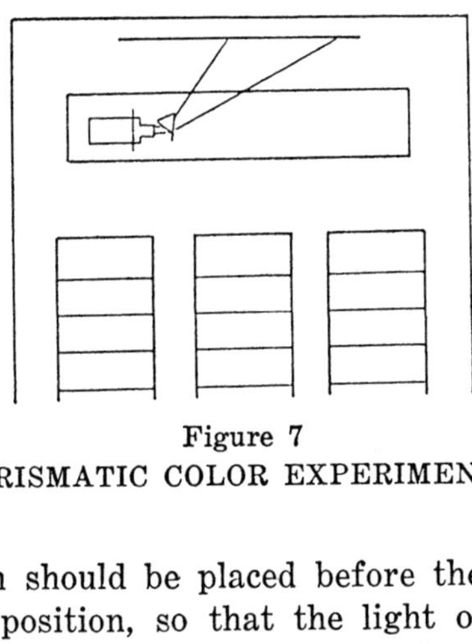

Figure 7
PRISMATIC COLOR EXPERIMENTS

A glass prism should be placed before the objective lens in a vertical position, so that the light of the projector passes through it and is bent sideways by refraction. The slide carrier is taken out, so that the space can be used to insert various objects. A pencil held in the space in a vertical position, with the objective lens adjusted to give a sharp shadow of it on the screen, will appear to have one of its vertical edges in yellow and red and the other in blue. Replacing the pencil by a knife, a pair of scissors, a comb, or particularly a twig with leaves or needles will provide a large variety of studies of colored edges. If the slide-carrier is returned to the projector, slides can be inserted and will appear on the screen with colored edges if projected through the prism. Particularly good results are obtained with slides of geometrical drawings that have alternate black and white areas.

We should not stop at the mere registering of the various color phenomena, but proceed to a realization of the conditions that will result in the appearance of the different colors. To this end we suggest inserting pieces of drawing paper into the slide-carrier from which have been cut a circle, a triangle and a square, using simple forms to simplify observation. With the piece that projects a white circle on a black background there is no color in the highest and lowest part of the circle. The strongest coloring appears to the left and to the right, diminishing towards the top with gradual transitions. On one side there will be yellow and red and on the other blue. With a white square resting on its base and with a black background, there will be no colors on its lower and upper bases. The vertical sides will show strong coloring, one in yellow and red, the other in blue. With a white triangle on a black background there will be no color along its base, but its other sides will appear in yellow and red, and in blue. A still further simplification of the conditions at hand will be achieved by sliding a piece of drawing paper into the space of the slide-carrier. The same piece of paper moved in from one side may show an edge of yellow and red, and from the other side of blue. By turning the prism to different positions the light passing through it will appear in turn upon the ceiling, upon one of the walls of the room, then upon the floor. How can we predict which color will appear on a given edge with a given position of the prism? The appearance of the colors depends upon the direction of the deviation through refrac-

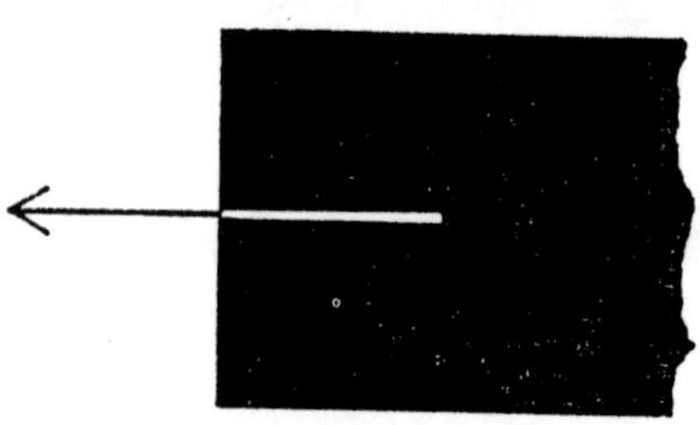

Figure 8
YELLOW AND RED
COLORED EDGE

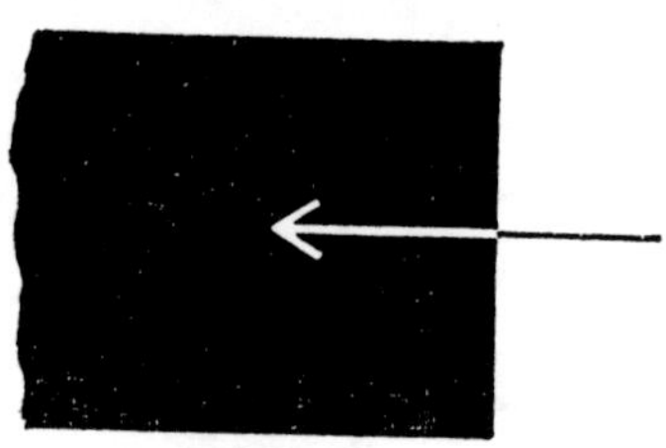

Figure 9
BLUE
COLORED EDGE

tion. In Figure 8 the arrow indicates the supposed direction of the optical deviation. Note that it reaches from a dark into a light field. In Figure 9 the arrow also indicates the supposed direction of the refraction, but now it reaches from a light into a dark field. The arrow-head of Figure 8 is drawn with dark lines on a white background and in Figure 9 with white lines on a dark background. The students will remember the darkening effect on the white sunlight, creating the sunset colors and the effect of light against a dark background resulting in the blue of the sky. One will try the rule of the arrows in different directions between white and black and check the results with the observation. The rule also applies in cases of looking through a prism and comparing the direction of the deviation through refraction with the colored edges. There is a multitude of observation to be made, and they all are in conformity with the described relationship between deviation and color. It provides examples of the scientific procedure of activating the mind within the multitude of observable facts.

GEOMETRICAL OPTICS

Following the optics of color, the next group of experiments leads us into geometrical optics. These experiments can be carried out with no more equipment than two plane mirrors (if possible of 1×2 ft. size) and a candle. The two mirrors are placed on a table in vertical position, joined together at one of their vertical edges, leaving a wedge-like space between them. The setup is called an "angular mirror". A candle is placed in the space between the mirrors. When the mirrors have an angle of 60° between them and one places the candle at a point equally distant from the two mirrors, one will see six candles — the candle itself and five mirror images. They stand in equal distances from one another and are located along a circle. When the angular mirror is set up with an angle of 45° between the mirrors, one will see eight candles. With smaller angles between the mirrors the number of candles increases. One can predict the number of candles which will appear by dividing 360° by the number of degrees of the angle between the mirrors— for 60° it is $\frac{360}{60} = 6$, for 45° it is $\frac{360}{45} = 8$. Conversely the angle between the mirrors can be obtained from the number of candles seen in the circle. With ten candles it will be $\frac{360}{10} = 36$. When a candle is placed before an angular mirror in such a way that it stands closer to one mirror than to the other, one will again see a circle of candles and the number of candles will follow the same rule, but the candles will no longer stand at equal distances, but the distances will be alternately smaller and larger.

If one takes a third mirror and forms an equilateral triangle with three mirrors, their reflecting sides turned inside, and sets up a candle in the middle of the triangle, a triangular pattern of candles will appear extending outward without limit. Similar experiments with four or five mirrors will show distributions of squares or pentagons and each time their number will appear to be infinite.

With simple means such experiments demonstrate the close relation between optics and geometry. They rarely fail to make a strong impression on the students.

The next step will be further experiments with angular mirrors showing various polygons and transitions between them. One places the angular mirror on a piece of cloth or blotting paper and on it a strip of paper about 1/8th of an inch wide, symmetrically across the opening of the angular mirror. Looking into the mirror one will see the straight line of the strip extended to a complete polygon. If the angle between the mirrors is 60° it will be a regular hexagon (perspective view in Fig. 10).

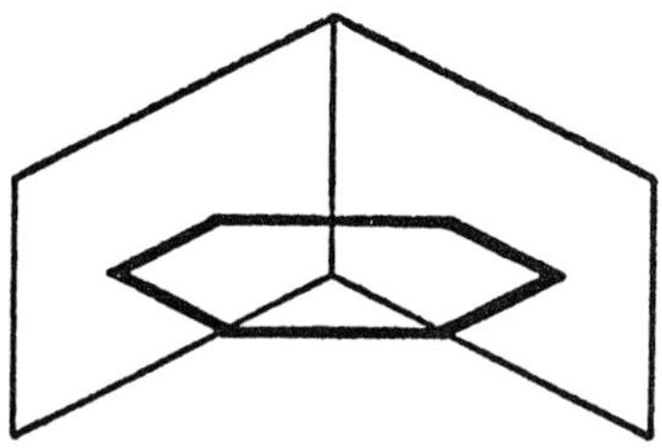

Figure 10
THE REGULAR HEXAGON IN AN ANGULAR MIRROR

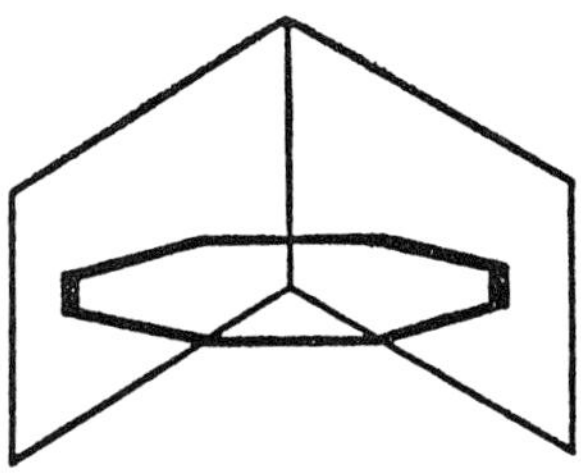

Figure 11
THE REGULAR OCTAGON IN AN ANGULAR MIRROR

If the angle between the mirrors is 45° one will see a regular octagon (perspective view in Fig. 11).

If, between the two mirrors, one places a cutout of an equilateral triangle of black or colored paper with an opening of 60° one will see a stellar hexagon (perspective view in Fig. 12).

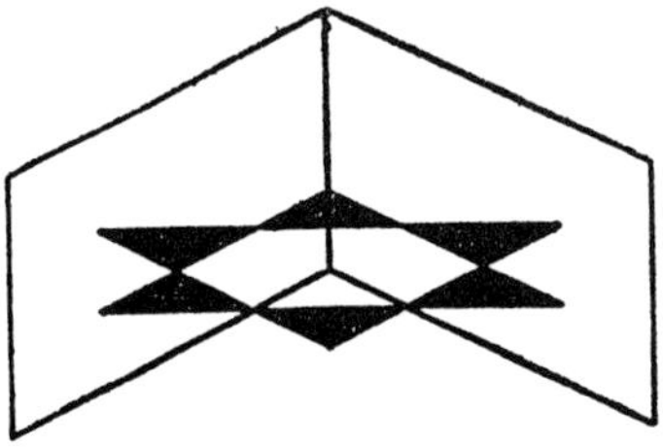

Figure 12
STELLAR HEXAGON IN AN ANGULAR MIRROR

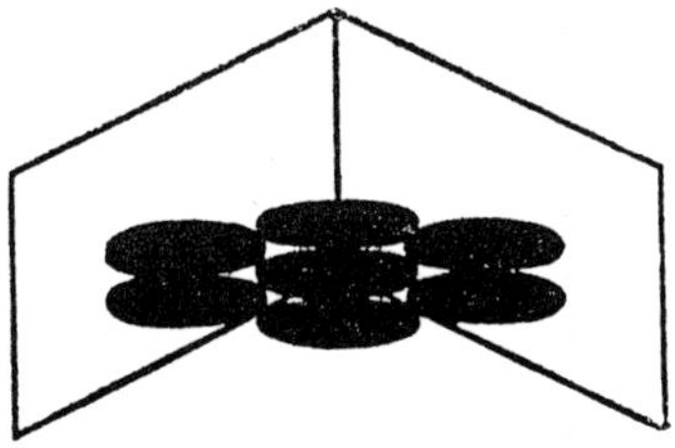

Figure 13
SEVEN CIRCLES IN AN ANGULAR MIRROR

A circular cutout placed between the angular mirror with the same opening will show 6 circles with the exact space for a seventh circle between them (perspective view in Fig. 13).

With several strips of paper and various openings between the mirrors a great variety of geometric forms can be obtained. An example with two strips of paper and an angular mirror of 360/16ths or 22 1/2° is shown in Fig. 14.

Figure 14
GEOMETRIC FORM IN AN ANGULAR MIRROR

Particularly stimulating are also experiments with geometric forms in motion with an angular mirror. An example is described with the following diagrams (Figs. 15 to 17).

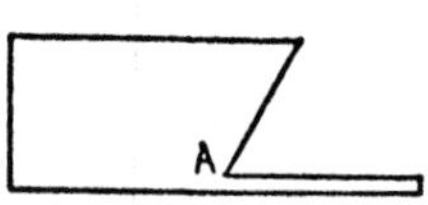

Figure 15

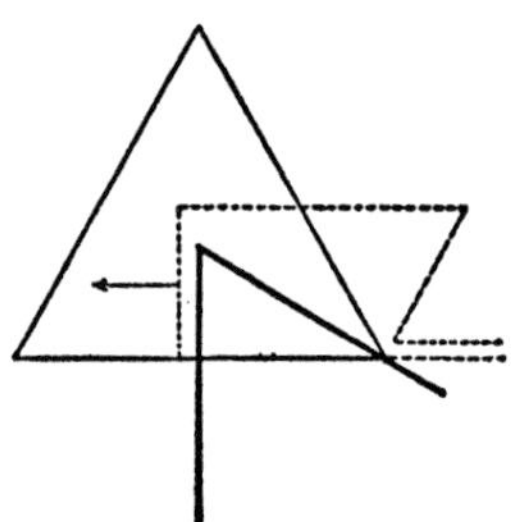

Figure 16

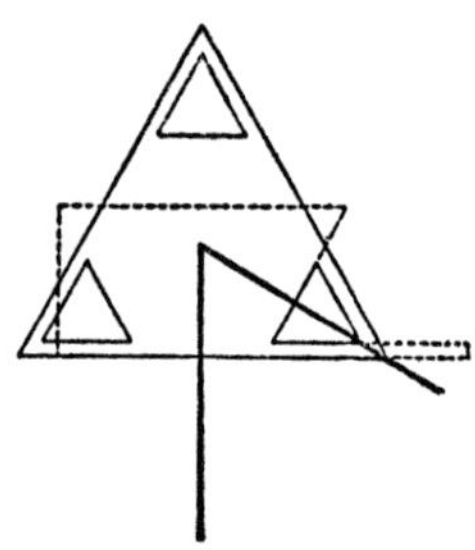

Figure 17

DESCRIBING EXPERIMENTS WITH GEOMETRIC FORMS IN MOTION

Cutting out the form of Fig. 15 and placing it under the angular mirror (position of the mirrors shown with stronger lines in Fig. 16; point A under one mirror) one obtains an equilateral triangle in the mirrors. Moving the cutout in the direction of the arrow in Fig. 16 until it reaches the position in Fig. 17 the mirror will show a hexagon inscribed in an equilateral triangle. It emerges in continuous motion from the triangle cutting off its corners. The diagrams obtained, as well as their continuations, are shown in a row in Fig. 18.

Figure 18
THE CHANGING FORMS OF THE MOVING DIAGRAM

If one adds another line to the moving cutout, as shown in Fig. 19, applying the same angular mirror and the same motion the forms of the moving diagram will be those of Fig. 20.

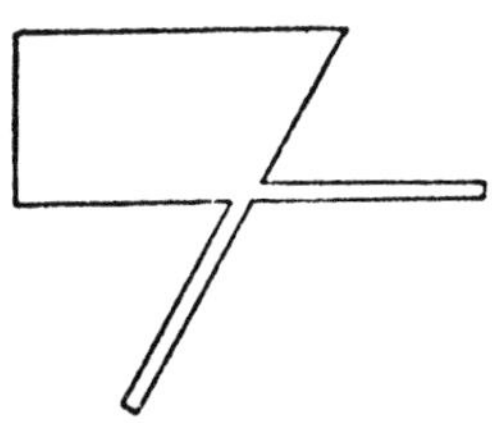

Figure 19

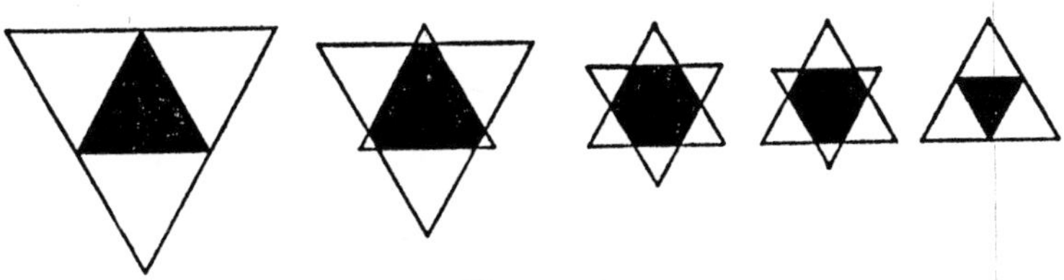

Figure 20
SEQUENCE OF FORMS OF THE SECOND MOVING DIAGRAM

Many further cutouts and motions will be conceived by the students. This calls on their initiative and imagination.

Following this, one will go further into details with the general principle of reflection. One will turn to a single plain mirror and hold a candle before it. If the candle is moved the image will show an accompanying motion. If the mirror is in a vertical plane and the candle moves without changing its distance from the mirror the accompanying motion will have the same direction.

When the candle moves upwards the image also moves upwards and does it with the same speed and for the same distance. When the candle moves to the left or to the right, the image follows it to the left and right, again with the same speed. All movements parallel to the plane of the mirror are accompanied by parallel movements. But if the candle is moved in a direction perpendicular to the mirror, its image moves forward. Then the mirror image no longer moves in the same, but in the opposite direction of the candle. If the candle moves in a line inclined to the plane of the mirror, the image also moves in an inclined direction, not parallel but symmetrical. The key to all these phenomena lies in the fact that the mirror image of any object is formed on the perpendicular from the point of the object to the plane of the mirror and extended as far behind the mirror as the object is located before it. This holds good

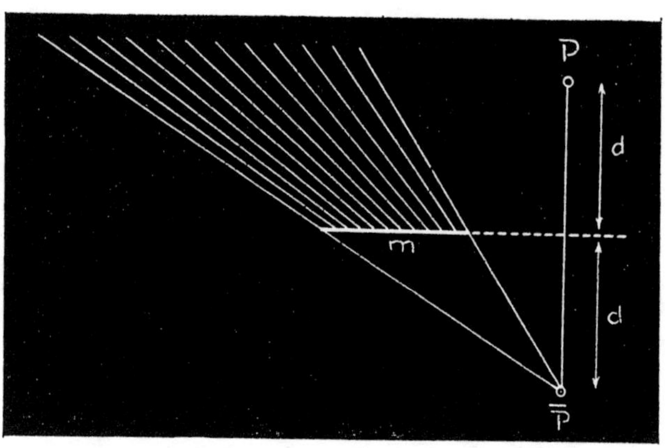

Figure 21
CONSTRUCTION OF A MIRROR IMAGE

even for points whose perpendiculars to the plane of the mirror are outside the limits of the mirror itself. In Figure 21 the stronger drawn line segment represents a mirror with the reflecting side turned upwards. The point P indicates the position of the candle which is located to the side of the mirror. The perpendicular passes through the mirror-plane to point $\overline{P}$ which is an equal distance along the perpendicular on the other side of the plane of the mirror and which is the apparent location of the mirror image. It is seen when one looks into the mirror from any point within the shaded space as though $\overline{P}$ were seen through a window instead of a mirror.

If one student will hold a mirror in different positions at various points of the classroom, and if another student will carry a candle about in the classroom, one can determine where a third student would have to stand in order to see the image of the candle in the mirror. Such exercises can also be reversed: One student holds the mirror in various positions and another student stands at a chosen place in the classroom. A third student will seek a position for the candle so that the second student will see it in the mirror.

In a third variation of this experiment one student will remain in his place, and the candle is placed at various points in the classroom while other students will have to find positions for the mirror so that the first student will see the mirror images.

After practice of this sort, we turn again to the angular mirror. Figure 22 marks the position of the two mirrors standing vertically above the lines to A and B with an angle of 60° between them. Their reflecting surfaces are turned towards P which marks the position of a candle. There will be a mirror image at P_1 in mirror A and another image at P_2 in mirror B. P_1 will have its image in mirror B at P_3, while P_2 in mirror A at P_4. The point P_3 is located before the mirror A (on the same side of its reflecting surface) and has its image in P_5. The point P_4, though behind the mirror A, is located before the mirror B and has its image also at P_5. Then there are no further images, as P_5 is located behind both mirrors.

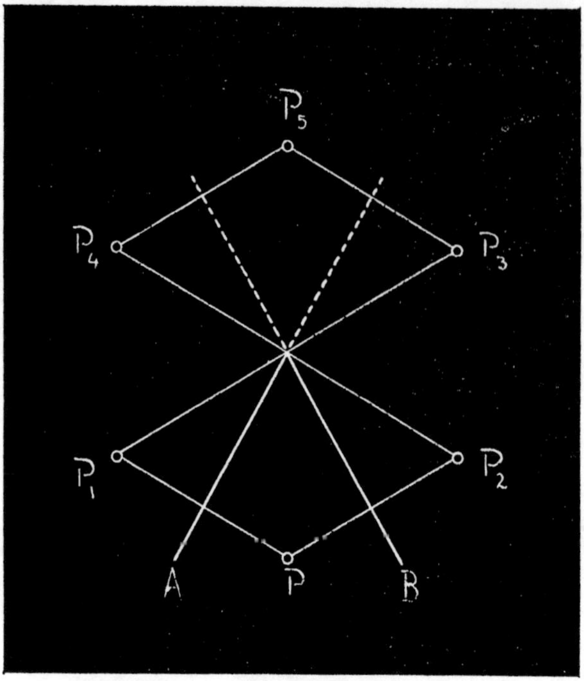

Figure 22
ANGULAR MIRROR OF 60°

The construction for a non-symmetrical position of P is drawn in Figure 23. The images appear in pairs, just as the previous experiment has shown.

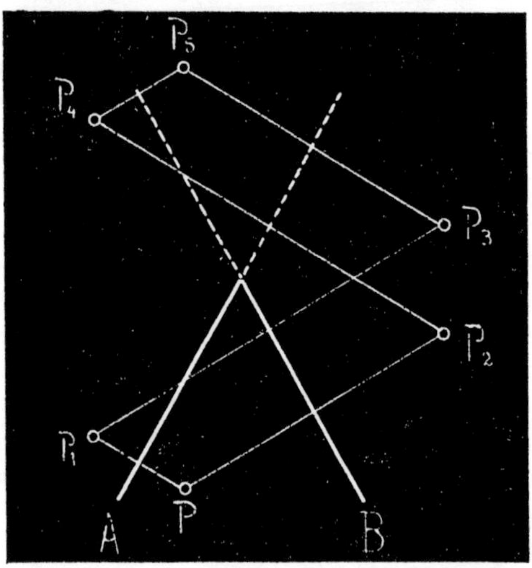

Figure 23
ANGULAR MIRROR OF 60° WITH A NON-SYMMETRICAL POSITION OF P

For an angular mirror of 30° we obtain $\frac{360}{30} = 12$ as the number of images (including the object). The corresponding illustration is in figure 24. The images are located along a circle. The circle does not appear as drawn by a compass, but along the dotted zig-zag lines of Figure 24.

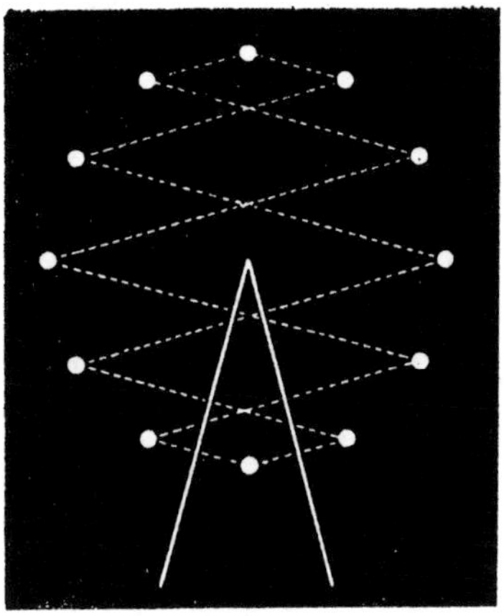

Figure 24
ANGULAR MIRROR OF 30°

With three mirrors set up in form of an equilateral triangle and a candle in their middle, three images are formed on the perpendicular lines to the three mirrors (Figure 25). Each image is located behind one mirror and at the same time before the two others. Therefore, further mirror images will be produced and the combined result is a hexagonal distribution of images over an unlimited area.

Analogous experiments and drawings can be extended to four, five and more mirrors with square, pentagonal, etc., groupings of images.

In these cases one geometrical principle led to the various figures. Another geometrical principle can also be found in connection with the reflection of plane mirrors. In a darkened room a slide projector is placed in front of the class, at one side of the room, and with its light projected across the demonstration table. Inserted in the slide-carrier is a piece of cardboard in which a circle has been cut out about the size of a dime, allowing the light to pass on to a mirror. The light is made visible in the air by means

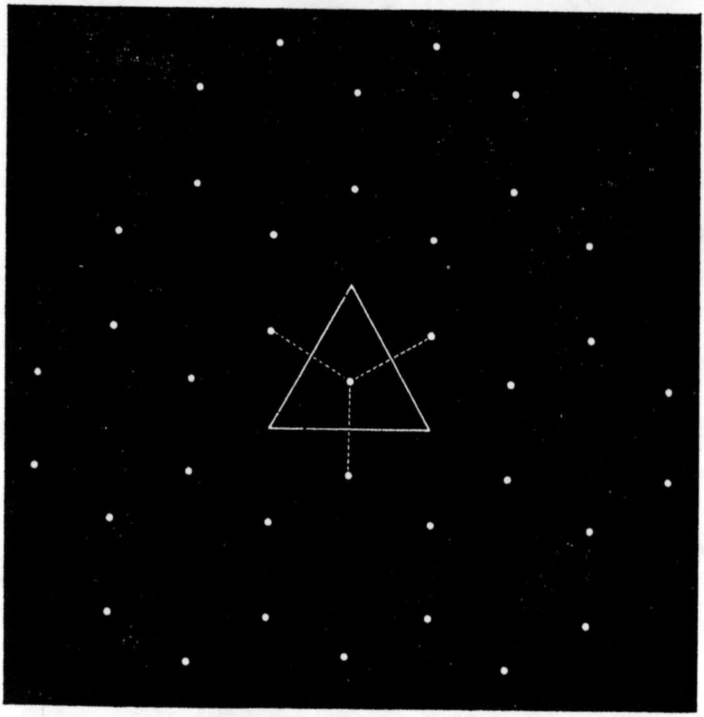

Fig. 25—THREE MIRRORS FORMING AN EQUILATERAL TRIANGLE

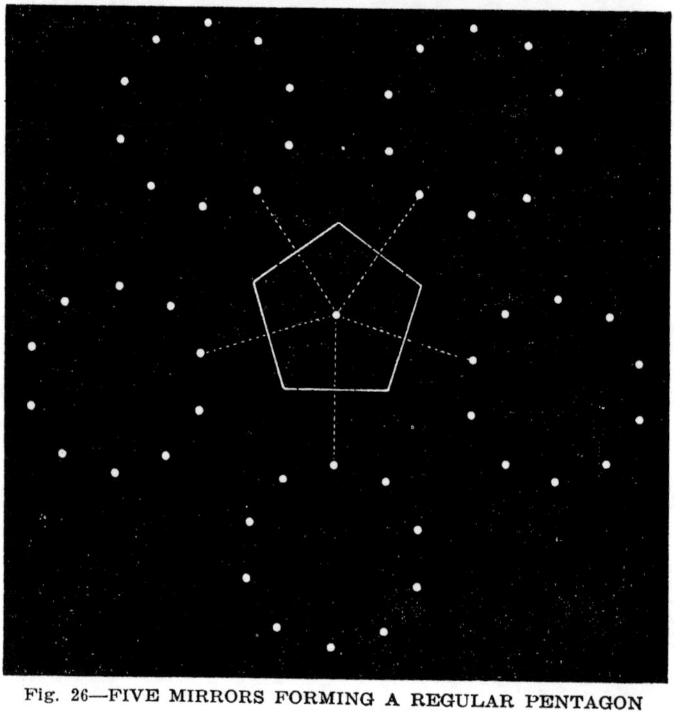

Fig. 26—FIVE MIRRORS FORMING A REGULAR PENTAGON

of smoke candles. Four to six smoke candles fixed with wax on a little board can be moved about the space over the demonstration table and soon the air will clearly show a horizontal line of light across the room. If then a plane mirror is held so that it intercepts this line, it will be bent back by reflection. Varying the angle of the mirror will change the angle of reflection. If the mirror is turned while the light shines upon it and the changing reflection is observed for a time, then one will be able to predict the reflected direction and formulate the law of reflection: the angle between the line of the incident light and the mirror equals the angle between the line of the reflected light and the mirror. The same fact can also be expressed with regard to the angles between the lines of light and the perpendicular erected on the mirror at the point of incidence. This latter method is particularly useful when the mirror is turned in all three dimensions, sideways as well as up and down and forwards and backwards. The experiments can be continued with different cardboard cuts inserted in the slide projector that will form two or more parallel lines of light, and with two or three mirrors set up for repeated reflection. Thus we can draw lines of light across the room much as we draw lines with pencils and paper.

A second medium in which the lines of reflection can be studied is water. For this a glass aquarium is filled with water, and a line of light from a projector set up to pass through it. A mirror placed in its path under the water will show that the reflection proceeds within the water in the same way as it does within air. If light is reflected from under the water towards its surface and it arrives there under a flat angle, it will be reflected downward from the surface.

The experiments in reflection can be summed up in the diagram of Figure 27. From a point O various lines of light are drawn down to a mirror m and their reflected lines are constructed. The latter are extended beyond the mirror, where all meet in the point I which is as far behind the mirror as the point O is before it. If O represents an object from which light emanates, the point I represents the mirror-image. Thus the two geometrical constructions of the law of reflection, the transfer of the angles, together

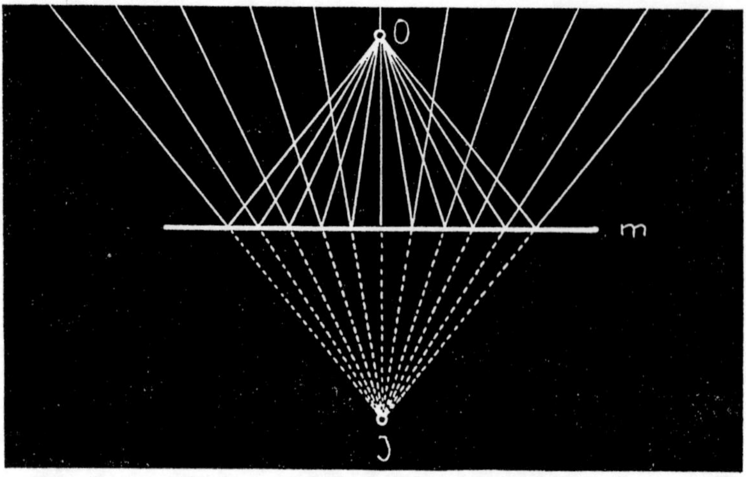

Figure 27
THE LAW OF REFLECTION

with the projection of the mirror-image on a perpendicular line, at a point as far behind the mirror as the object is before it, are summed up in one illustration.

By making the lines of light visible in the air, as well as in the water, we can also show how the light passes from the air into the water and from the water into the air and demonstrate the change of angles through refraction. Thus we arrive at a link between geometrical optics and the optics of color as it has been followed in the previous chapter.

The school plan then continues with mechanics for the 7th Grade. This corresponds to the progressively realistic attitudes of students of this age. Mechanics is taken up with a study of machinery. One will bring in mechanical devices, such as a lawn mower, tools of the workshop, gadgets of the kitchen and will discuss the workings of a car, etc. Whenever the school is near a farm some examples of farm machinery offer themselves particularly well, as their functioning can readily be seen. One will study the different kinds of motions and their transformations into one another. From there one will proceed to the respective forces, to the golden rules of mechanics, etc.

In the 8th Grade the mechanics of liquids and gases is added, as well as those sections of physics which have not yet been taken up, particularly electricity.

In the Senior High School the various sections of physics come in again with a different, more mathematical, treatment. In the 9th Grade, the emphasis is on the physics of heat; in the 10th Grade on mechanics of solids, liquids and gases; in the 11th Grade on electricity and in the 12th Grade on optics, with a general final survey.

THE JUNIOR HIGH PHYSICS LABORATORY

The kind of experimenting described for the introduction of physics in the Junior High grades calls for quite different laboratories than those required for High Schools or Colleges. For schools which include both Junior High and High School two different physics laboratories should be set up in order to do justice to the respective needs. In the Junior High laboratory there should be equipment for experiments on the border line between the artistic and scientific fields, such as the Glockenspiel, sonometers, water colors, colored glass, etc. The quality of impressions conveyed to the students at this level is even more important than the quantitative aspect. Good musical equipment and good colors are essential. Also there should be equipment such as smoke-candles to perform experiments that will involve the entire classroom, not confining them to the demonstration table. There should be plenty of simple materials such as different colored crepe paper, as well as wires, plates, rods, different types of wood to be examined for their sound. Then tools and materials such as cardboards, glassware, etc., are used.

A proper laboratory of this kind can be a real stimulus and source of ideas for the teacher in preparing his physics unit. It will help to make instruction the kind of experience for the student which is attuned to his own interests and not a mere copy of College or High School work. A special art of experimenting emerges from it for the Physics of this Age.

SUMMARY

THE BALANCE BETWEEN ART AND SCIENCE

The time usually allotted to art in a school plan is one double period a week. When the period starts the child asks: "What shall I paint?" The teacher makes suggestions and when one of them strikes the child's imagination he or she will set to work. The double period passes by quickly, the more so since a considerable part of it has already been spent in the initial discussion. One week later, with all the contents of the week having made their claims on the children's interest the thread is lost and again there is the question; "What shall I paint?" The cycle starts anew. The procedure—sometimes continued year in and year out—cannot bring much satisfaction either to the child or to the art teacher. The teacher feels that his subject plays but a secondary role in the weekly plan, reflecting the role that art itself is often playing in life to-day. Does this do justice to art and to its task in education?

In the Waldorf School Plan, art is made a major subject. In the elementary school years it is given by the group teacher and brought into close contact with practically every subject. In the Junior and Senior High School art is taught in double periods every day for continued units of three weeks. Thus the interest aroused on the preceding day is taken up on the following. There is a well-prepared beginning, a climax, and a full stop. A substantial piece of work can be completed in a surveyable time span. The teacher and the child feel the satisfaction of an achievement.

Still this is not all that the Waldorf School Plan has provided in regard to art. Even an alive and successful teaching of art which is isolated from the other school work does not fulfill its task. Friedrich von Schiller said, "Only through the door of beauty can you enter the kingdom of knowledge." This is carried through in the Waldorf School Plan, and acoustics, for instance, is introduced through music and the optics of color through painting, as it has been described in the previous chapters.

All boys and girls in the Waldorf Schools have singing and music beginning in the Nursery and Kindergarten and continuing through the elementary grades. In the First Grade this includes singing and playing on the block flutes as required activities for all children, and in the following grades it is continued. Before the Sixth Grade all children have acquired a knowledge of musical intervals, of the keyboard of the piano, and of the different major and minor keys and of their respective notations. Up to the Sixth Grade the musical intervals, as well as the various keys, stand for experiences of specific musical qualities. Then in the Sixth Grade the students are led to realize that these intervals, as well as the keys, also have other sides to them, connections with measurements and numbers. Anyone, even with a relatively poor musical development, but knowing that an octave is made by the tones of a string at half of its length will be able to produce an octave as accurately as it could be done by the keenest musical ear. The scientific facts added to art open up new possibilities.

The described approach to acoustics is backed by actual historical development. Historically the step from music to acoustics was taken by the Pythagorean School in the early Greek civilization (6th Century B.C.). The fact that number relationships exist in connection with music made a deep impression and led to an entire philosophy of life. Inmost secrets of life can be expressed in music and music is permeated by number relations. One begins to understand the Pythagorean School's consideration of numbers as the root of all existence.

The students of the Sixth Grade are in a period of transition between two approaches to life. While in elementary school they have an idealistic approach whereas in the Sixth Grade they pass on to a realistic one. This transition is at the basis of the step from Art to Science. The school plan is tuned to what goes on within the student. In these occurrences the individual somehow repeats the development of the race. The biogenetic law holds good not only for the development of the body but also of the mind.

With regard to color, all children of the Waldorf Schools have had their experiences from the Nursery and Kindergarten upwards. First they handle their water colors without reference to observations in nature and gain their experiences in the realm of color itself. In Elementary school, painting is carried on from grade to grade. Beginning with the Sixth Grade observations of color in nature are systematically taken up. The students are made aware of how various ranges of mountains, some nearer and some farther away, show distinct color sequences. The nearest wooded slopes stand out darker and with a more varied green. The farther away the mountains are, the lighter they appear and they show a gradual approach to the blue of the sky with increasing distances. The students paint pictures making use of these color sequences. Similar exercises in color perspective may be practiced with respect to the golden slopes of the California mountains. Their yellow becomes paler in the distance and gradually merges into the blue of the sky. One may also turn to the sea and observe how the darker blue of the water in the foreground becomes lighter in the distance and again approaches the sky-blue. The color of the sky above shows analogous changes. Its blue is not uniform from the various angles at which we look up into it. The sky vertically above us has a more intense and darker color than towards the horizon. All of these sequences vary with different weather conditions; they change from daylight to twilight and change with various geographical latitudes, from polar to tropic countries. These observations of the changing colors will be carried on to those changes which occur with the colors of different objects under different conditions of light. The same object in full daylight will show a different color than it will in the evening light. On its side turned towards the light, its color differs from the one that is in shadow. All this is followed up through various painting exercises. It leads to the application of the complementary colors and exactly to the point where the transition from painting to the optics of color is made, as previously described.

The Waldorf School Plan also contains for the Sixth Grade an introduction to geometry. It starts with the regular forms and the students draw various diagrams and learn of regular triangles, squares, regular pentagons, hexagons, and also of regular polygons with higher numbers of sides, etc. They learn of stellar polygons and geometric progressions. The building up of their skill in handling the drawing instruments goes hand in hand with their progress of learning. With their exercises the dividing of a circle into equal parts plays a major role. All this is at the same time the very preparation for geometrical optics. Just as the optics of color is derived from painting, so geometrical optics starts with geometrical forms. Then it proceeds to the observing of forms in our surroundings and finally meets with the laws of nature in optics. In both instances, with color and with geometry, the way leads from within, outwards, starting from a reviving of one's own activity and then turning to the surroundings. Thus the closest link between the inner life and the outer observation is established. Instead of a cleavage between inner and outer experience an integrated harmony is achieved.

What has been omitted in the preceding approach should now be mentioned. Middle C has 250 vibrations per second, and a string which gives a tone an octave higher has double the number of vibrations. The musical intervals have not been introduced in reference to the ratios between their numbers of vibrations, but rather in reference to lengths of the strings. The reason is that the lengths of strings remain within the realm of immediate observation. For the teaching of physics, particularly for this age level, it is of special importance to make a careful discrimination between observable facts, and other elements which go beyond the immediate experience. For different mental situations the world makes sense ever anew. It makes sense for the Kindergarten child, it makes sense for the primitive in Africa, it makes sense for our realistic age, and it makes sense for the scientist. We inject disturbing elements by assuming that we would have to step beyond our specific realm in order to answer our questions. To talk of wave lengths of light, of atoms and electrons in order to answer the questions of the realistic age has a negative effect. Skepticism on the one hand and dogmatism on the other are the consequences. The student will pass on to a later period in his life more successfully if he has been firmly grounded in the previous one. One may argue: "but how would one explain electricity without speaking of electrons?" The answer is: "there is plenty to be told about electricity which is clearly accessible to student's observation without recourse to any theoretical elements." This puts an interesting and stimulating task before us. Having written a physics treatise in three volumes with the emphasis: PHYSICS AS PURE PHENOMENOLOGY,* the author has demonstrated that this is possible. Many more young people could find their way into science and find a sound relationship to it. Instead they often find themselves overwhelmed by it and either lose interest and turn away from it or learn to accept it dogmatically without a personal relationship.

The balance between, and the merging of, the creativeness of art and the background of facts of the sciences set a real goal, an ideal, and every effort made towards it bears fruit for the individual student, as well as for the structure of our present civilization.

* (in German)